FREIGHT YARDS

TRAINS

Lynn M. Stone

The Rourke Corporation, Inc.
Vero Beach, Florida 32964

PHOTO CREDITS: All photos © Lynn M. Stone

ACKNOWLEDGEMENT: The author thanks the Union Pacific Railroad and its employees for assistance in the preparation of photos for this book.

PRODUCED BY:
East Coast Studios, Merritt Island, Florida

EDITORIAL SERVICES:
Penworthy Learning Systems

Library of Congress Cataloging-in-Publication Data

Stone, Lynn M.
   Freight yards / by Lynn M. Stone
     p. cm. — (Trains)
   Summary: Describes how freight yards build freight trains, by sorting the cars onto sidings and coupling them together into new trains.
   ISBN 0-86593-522-X
   1. Railroads Juvenile literature. 2. Railroads—Yards Juvenile literature
3. Railroads—Freight Juvenile literature. [1. Railroads 2. Railroads—Trains]
I. Title. II. Series: Stone, Lynn M. Trains.
TF148.S87 1999
385.3'14—dc21
                                       99-13277
                                         CIP

TABLE OF CONTENTS

Freight Yards   5
Freight Trains   6
Building a Freight Train   11
The Hump   16
Freight Yards at Work   22
Glossary   23
Index   24
Further Reading   24

FREIGHT YARDS

A railroad freight yard is a loud, busy place. Railroad **locomotives** (LO kuh MO tivz) pulling lines of freight cars rumble around the yards.

Freight cars haul almost anything that needs to be moved from one place to another. Freight can be such things as steel, coal, oil, lumber, refrigerators, grain, or automobiles.

A big freight yard does many jobs for the **railroad** (RAYL rod). Its main purpose is to put lines of freight cars together and take them apart.

Freight yards bustle with the activity of locomotives and train cars on several tracks.

FREIGHT TRAINS

A freight train is made up of freight cars and one or more locomotives. Trains are owned by railroads. A railroad's job is to haul goods, or products, on its rails. A company that wants to ship lumber, for example, from Oregon to Illinois may choose to hire a railroad for the job.

A locomotive hauls its freight cars to one or more locations. The people who work in the freight yard decide which cars should be put onto which train.

This lumber company in Oregon will ship its freight eastward by railroad.

Freight cars and locomotives are joined to each other with steel **couplers** (KUP lerz). The couplers snap shut like strong jaws. After the cars are coupled, or connected, the freight train is sent from the yard to wherever it is going.

Every day, some 10,000 freight trains travel across North America. Some of these trains are over two miles (3 kilometers) long. They may have as many as 200 cars. The average freight train has about 70 cars.

An eastbound Union Pacific freight races through Maple Park, Illinois, on its route to Chicago.

BUILDING A FREIGHT TRAIN

A freight yard has dozens of short lengths of track called **sidings** (SIE dingz). Freight cars are sorted onto sidings by type. A group of tank cars, for example, can be put together on a siding. On another siding, workers can put boxcars, auto cars, or other types of freight cars.

A Burlington Northern switcher working in a "flat yard"—a yard without a hump—pulls a short line of mixed freight cars.

A trainman climbs aboard a switcher in Union Pacific's Chicago yard. The trainman's orange wrap shows one way that railroads stress safety.

Sidings give a railroad places to park and organize its cars.

A train is put together with cars that will be going in the same direction. Sometimes an entire train is going to one place. Often, though, groups of cars are dropped at places along a route.

At the freight yard, locomotives called switchers push and pull cars onto and off sidings. The switchers help gather the right cars to form a "new" train that will leave the yard.

Meanwhile, trains coming into the yard are taken apart. The cars are put onto sidings for later use.

A line of locomotives stands ready for duty at a Union Pacific yard. Workers in the tower (background) oversee traffic in the yard.

THE HUMP

Big freight yards use Mother Nature as well as locomotives to help move train cars. Mother Nature in this case is gravity.

The force of gravity allows things to roll downhill. Some freight yards, which are also known as classification yards, have a hill, or hump. The hump helps the railroad sort its cars and build "new" trains.

At the top of the hump, a freight car or small group of cars is uncoupled from the original train. The car or cars are sent on tracks down the hump. Each car rolls easily downhill.

A quartet of covered hoppers rolls down the hump to a siding.

Several sidings are below the hump. Each siding holds cars going to a certain place. A hump can direct some 2,000 cars each day onto sidings.

A controller in a tower near the hump directs each car to one of the sidings. Computers help the controller. The controller can change which siding is open by flipping an electrical switch in the railroad tracks. A switch allows a car, or an entire train, to move from one set of rails to another.

The train cars rolling down a hump are slowed by **retarders** (ri TAHRD erz). Retarders are built into the tracks. They are controlled by computers.

As a car reaches its siding, it is traveling just fast enough to couple with the car ahead of it on the siding. Now the car has been **classified** (KLAS uh fied), or sorted, into the right group.

In freight yards without humps, switchers do all the work of moving cars around. Freight yards that use humps to classify cars are often called hump yards.

A railroad worker checks the wheelbox of a covered hopper car on a yard siding.

FREIGHT YARDS AT WORK

The workers in freight yard towers operate radios and computers. The workers stay in contact with train engineers and oversee the work of the yard.

On the ground, at track level, some workers run the trains. An engineer operates the locomotive. A conductor, who rides with the engineer, checks on the train's condition.

Other workers in a freight yard repair cars and engines. Still others work in offices and keep track of sales and shipments.

GLOSSARY

classified (KLAS uh fied) — having been put into the correct group or class

coupler (KUP ler) — a handlike steel device by which railroad cars and locomotives can be connected, or coupled, and uncoupled

locomotive (LO kuh MO tiv) — a power plant or engine on wheels used to push or pull railroad cars; a train engine

railroad (RAYL rod) — a company that owns and operates trains to carry passengers or freight

retarder (ri TAHRD er) — a device built into railroad tracks and used to slow down freight cars being sorted

siding (SIE ding) — a short length of railroad track, apart from the main track, on which a train may be safely parked

INDEX

cars, freight   5, 6, 9, 11, 16, 20
computers   19, 20, 22
conductor   22
controller   19
couplers   9
engineers   22
freight   5
freight yards   5, 6, 11, 14, 16, 20
hump   16, 19, 20
hump yards   20
locomotives   5, 6, 9, 16

North America   9
railroads   5, 6
rails   6, 19
sidings   11, 14
switch   19
switchers   14, 20
tower   19, 22
tracks   16, 19, 20
train   6, 9, 14, 16, 19, 20
   freight   6, 9

FURTHER READING

Find out more about trains with these helpful books and information sites:

Riley, C.J. *The Encyclopedia of Trains and Locomotives.* Metro Books, 1995

Association of American Railroads online at www.aar.org
California State Railroad Museum online at www.csrmf.org
Union Pacific Railroad online at http://www.uprr.com